# W. RUTH KOZAK

---

# SONGS FOR ERATO

# Table of Contents

*Dedicated to Erato, Muse of Poetry*

# Odes to the Muse of Poetry

*"My words have wings
made of air
words good to hear.
I sing them
to please you."*
– Lyric poet Sappho, known as the 10th Muse. 500 BC

## Midnight Muse

My Muse comes after midnight

Nudges me awake,

whispers urgently:

"Get up! Write!"

I curse her,

stumble across the dark room,

search for matches,

light the candle wick.

Where has she been in the daylight?

How many hours did I want for her,

listening for her voice?

"Where were you?" I ask.

'Was it your voice I heard

while I daydreamed in the sun?

Or was it only the sound

of sheep bells

on the mountain?"

"Write!" she demands. "Write!"

And I know if I wait til morning

the words she whispers to me

will be extinguished

like this candle flame

as I snuff it out.


*Written while living in a shepherd's cottage, Lala, Evvia, Greece.*

## Looking for the Muse

The Muse doesn't like the heat.

When Helios scorches the earth

hot as Hades realm,

She lifts her skirts

and runs to Poseidon's cooling embrace.

I tread Athens' burning pavements

looking for her,

dare not climb the Sacred Rock,

instead, take refuge on the Aegean's sandy sore.

Here, where gentle zephyrs cool the air.

The Muse breathes, sighs, speaks to me.


*Athens, September 2010.*

# Poems for Athena

## Athena

Athena! You seductress,

You fallen angel!

Your shining crown is tarnished;

Your ancient beauty has faded.

But you are still

as enchanting as you were

in your golden days.

You tease me, lure me.

Like a Corinthian whore

you whisper sweet promises to me.

I am intoxicated by the

fragrant garlands you wear;

the jasmine, *niktaria* and Daphne.

I taste the honey of your kiss.

I dance to the throbbing of your music.

I am your captive, Athena,

held in your seething embrace.

You have charmed me, seduced me.

I am caught in your spell,

Athena!


*Athens, 1982*

## Socrates' Prison

In this quiet courtyard

Where you spent your final hours

little birds

Sing from the olive trees.


Here, among the tumbled rocks

a crimson poppy blooms

as though

it sprang from your blood.


*Athens Agora*

## Under the Wild Pepper Tree

There was an atrium here once,

where the wild pepper tree

guarded a garden of flowers –

*nectaria* and jasmine, and little flowers,

gold as stars,

that twinkled among the vines.

The cool marble of the pillars shaded this place.

We used to sit here in the sunshine

drowsing away the afternoons

while you played your lyre,

sang of the forest and mountains and sea.

The same wind rustles the pods today.

The same voices echo gaily from the Acropolis.

Now you are gone

and I sit here waiting to hear your music.

But there is only the whisper of the wind

rustling the pods of the wild pepper tree.


Under the wild pepper tree

you sang a song about jasmine and love,

while the night breeze

signed through the branches

scatter the dried pods

to the ground.


The night we made love

under the wild pepper tree

your song echoed across the Agora

and the Acropolis was illuminated

with golden light.


The day I sat alone

under the wild pepper tree

I listened for the song about jasmine

but heard only the birds

and the sighing of the trees

and the scuttling of the dried pods

as they scattered  to the ground

in the place where we made love.


After the rain,

the birds sing in the laurel

while under the wild pepper tree

I wait,

wishing I could hear your song.

But years have passed since then,

and in the moonlight

under the Acropolis,

another man made love to me.

The words he spoke

were more beautiful

than your song about the jasmine.

But I cannot forget you.

You brought me here

to this secret place

where the breeze

scatters the pepper pods

and they fall, sighing,

at my feet.

*Athens Agora , October 1979*

## Ode to the Young Kouroi

In the museum

the marble *kouros*

stands erect

long locks brushing his shoulders,

eyes gazing into

an unknown future.

I see them, today's *kouroi,*

standing on a street corners,

holding machine guns

in clenched fists.

Is this what has become of

the young men

who once lolled in Plaka Square

chatting up tourist girls

stealing hearts?

Are these guns the new *kamakis?*

Is the broken glass they tread on

from shattered windows?

Instead of plundering hearts

in foreign ports

do they arrest roving marauders

who plunder their city?

They look young enough to be my

grandson, barely out of college

perhaps recruited from army duties.

Do they, like their fathers,

dance like Zorba on broken plates,

aim their golden arrows

into the hearts of tourist girls?

Like the museum kouros

these boys face an unknown future

These beautiful

bronze-skinned kouroi

are the new

protectors of Athens

They are Greeks

survivors, resilient, daring,

the heroes of a new generation.


*Athens, 2010*

## Lament for the Old Ones

What has happened to those

beautiful Greek boys,

those Adonis who used to turn

our heads and steal our hearts.

Where are the Zorbas

who danced with passion

on broken plates

and later broke our hearts?

Have they all become these

bald, gray-haired, unshaven men

who laze away their days at *kafeneions*

bemoaning the state of the economy,

reminiscing of the days

they sailed boldly into foreign ports

like pirates,

seducing the local girls

with their charms?

They used to loll in Plaka Square,

*kamakis* poised,

enough of them

to make a girl's head dizzy,

oozing their Mediterranean charm.

I see only tired old men,

ancient as their myths.

Where are those beautiful gods?

Where is Eros

Who struck our hearts with

His golden arrows.

Now they work in tavernas

on hot summer days

slogging beer and souvlaki to tourists

while I sit and watch

remembering those golden days

when Plaka Square was filled

with laughter and love.


*A* kamaki *is a 3-pronged trident used for fishing.*

*Plaka Square, August 2010*

# The Ghosts of Vironos Street

I walk past 14 Vironos,

touch the gate

recall my life there:

Kyria Dina's scarlet geraniums,

the little *spitaki* in the courtyard

Occupied by writers, artists.

Robbie sipping *krasi*

expounding on his life

as an Argentine exile

So much flotsam tossed on

Aegean shores.


At the Dirty Corner

( named because of the dust of the excavation)

stands the tripod monument of Lysistratis,

won by a chorus at the Dionysus Theatre,

when this was ancient Athen's theatre district.


Poets lived here: Byron, Shelley

(Vironos is Byron's Street).

**This is where we lived the Greek** *zoe*

This is where we bared our passions

to the passersby.

Dramas were enacted on this Corner,

relationships begun and ended.

Once I threw a wine glass at Mikalis.

Missed.


On winter nights

we sat inside the milk shop

huddled around a heater

sipping Metaxa brandy.

The Katherine Hepburn of the Corner,

and her maniac Canadian boyfriend,

Mary Rogers, the faded debutante,

always with a bottle of vodka in her handbag

and an entourage of toy-boys in tow.

Robbie, my soul-mate,

telling stories about

his beloved Buenos Aires.

We shared our lives on that Corner,

knew each other's secrets

and sorrows.


Now the milk shop is a ritzy café-bar

the dust of the excavation

swept away

along with the memories

Old friends have disappeared,'

left for other places,

some taken too soon.

Yet their spirits linger still.


I wonder if the tourists who sit here

sipping frappe and wine

know this Corner's history?

Can they feel the presence

of the ghosts?


When I pass the Corner,

I hear echoes of voices past,

stop by Kyria Dina's iron gate

wishing it would open again,

to let me into the sunny courtyard

and find Roberto at his easel

waiting to hear my day's adventures


Last night as I walked,

out of Vironos Street

across the Areopagitou,

I saw him, Robbie,

walking in his slow amble

toward me.

I recognized his slender frame,

the grey pony-tail and beard.

He looked up, caught my eyes.

As I passed, I heard him say

in his mischievous way:

29.

"Misbehave!"

Then, like a shadow,

He was gone.

So many memories

on Vironos Street

and that little corner of Plaka.

Yes, the ghosts are there


I see them, feel their presence

hear their laughter as I pass by.


*Athens, Plaka, September 2010*

## The Bouzouki Dancers

I wonder if when they dance

they imagine they are seagulls

skimming over the white

crests of waves

touching down lightly

in a spray of silver mist,

gliding,

swooping

soaring again

up into the sun.

# Adonis

You seduce me, Adonis,

with your dazzling smile.

You, bronze god

with hair as black as Apollo's raven

and the emerald sea in your eyes,

You are like the pretty flowers

on a thorn bush.

I am intoxicated

by your fragrance,

enchanted by your beauty,

but when I hold you too close

 your thorns leave their scars

on my heart.

## In the National Gardens

In the garden cicadas trill from the trees.

People stroll to and fro, others sit on shaded benches.

Tall palms line the quiet pathways, flowers bloom in colorful plots.

This was once the King's Botanical Garden, reserved for royalty.

Now it's the people's Park

It used to be much grander: duck ponds, deer, exotic birds,

a pathetic old lion in a round cage.

Once I walked through every day, admired rose beds

Paused in the shade to watch white ducks paddle in the pond.


Today, the ducks are gone

 the pond is empty, coated with green sludge.

Where are the *papakia*?


No *pak pak pak'* as excited children throw bread crusts.

Only tired pigeons squatting in the shade.

Now the people's park seems a lonely place

I hesitate to venture along the secluded paths.

Where are the cats today? The prowling strays

Who bask on the sunny lawns?

A woman used to come every day at noon

Lay food down on the stone fence.

Dozens of cats, tabbies, gingers, calicoes, greys, would line up

Waiting for their turn to savour the treats she brought.

I miss those cats, though these days they may have found another place to dine.

Today it's oddly quiet in the Garden

except for the chirring of cicadas

and the muted sounds of traffic on busy Amalias Street.

The park is desolate, shabby, the gardens sparse.


Flowers wilt in the parched soil, overgrown with weeds,

like the people, sucked dry by crooked politicians.


*papakia:* ducks

*Athens, September 2015*

# Haunted Tables

The tables are haunted at this sidewalk tavern.

Even though they are filled with tourists

The ghosts of the past still linger here.

Once across the street where the new museum
dominates,

There were apartments where friends once live:

Graham, the Englishman, and Lilian the Jewish
woman from New York

a houseful of Filipinos who worked at menial tasks

and an old souvlaki shop run by a kindly old gent we
called "Mr Souvlaki"


We'd sit here every night,

Roberto from Argentina, other friends from Norway
and Finland,

Swedes, Germans, English and American

Mingling with the Greeks who came

To sample Anna's delicious home-cooked meals.


There would always be laughter

and sometimes music when Dino played his
bouzouki.

Now the tables are still crowded,

but the people who come here are strangers –
tourists

drawn to the place by the tempting menu and
friendly ambience.

Robert, Graham have gone, died so soon.

Some like Lilian returned to the States,

Others have moved on, drop by only occasionally.


But in spite of the haunted tables,

I come here to cherish the memories,

All those nights I once spent here with my friends,

Recall the stories,

the laughter and the tears.

the dramas that unfolded here,

It is still, and always will be,


my favorite place to come in Athens.

The food is still good (recommended by Rick Steeves!)

And sometimes there even is music

Whenever Dino has time to play his bouzouki.


*At the To Kati Allo Taverna, Athens 2015.*

## Greek Drama

They have dramatic storms here in Greece.

Zeus thunders across the heavens in his chariot

Hurling fiery arrows.

Black clouds pour down torrents of rain on the island's sun-scorched earth,

The wind howls.

Waves crash on the beach.

On Hatzichristou Street, a woman paces,

outside the To Kati Allo tavern,

shouts angrily at a man who owes her money.


He calls her a *putana*.'

The drama escalates.

*"Fie! Fie"* the tavern owner warns.

"Leave! Leave!"

I hold my breath, waiting,

expecting her to lash out.

I know her wrath,

as formidable as Zeus's.

Then her son  intervenes.

His gentle diplomacy creates a lull in the storm,

calms the waves.

The angry woman drifts away

The storm is appeased.

# They Buried You in a Pauper's Grave

*for Robbie*

They buried you in a pauper's grave

with your paint brushes

I remember when you sat at your easel

in the courtyard

painting Mangas and prostitutes,

and Icon-like portraits of your lover.

Once you painted me, wearing my favourite magenta sweater.

The mermaid you gave me hangs on my bathroom wall.


They buried you in a pauper's grave.

Mike made the grave-marker

the back of an old wooden tavern chair

decorated with things an artist would use.

It might have been a chair you'd sat at

**those long hours in the** *plateia*

sipping wine while you discussed art and literature,

reminisced about your beloved Argentina.

They called you the philosopher of the Plaka.


They buried you in a paupers' grave.

Panayiotis planted flowers in the barren soil.

All around, the ground was scattered with pine-needles.

We stood around your grave, mourned your departure,

remembered your grace and dignity,

your intelligence and artistic talent.

I recall the first time I saw you,

when you came into the Sunset Bar,

a tall, blonde Adonis with sky-blue eyes.

I thought you were a movie star.

You were a Gemini, like me,

my soul-brother and companion.


They buried you in a pauper's grave.

I can't forget the times we sat and talked the night away,

all the days we spent together,

sunny days in the courtyard.

We sipped wine while you painted at your easel,

your ashtray overflowing with burned-out butts.

We listened to music: Shirley Basie, Edith Piaf.

Sometimes you cried when the songs made you sad.

Sometimes we cried together for all the me we'd loved before.

They  buried you in a pauper's grave.

Who will tend it now? Who will bring fresh flowers?

You have no family. Will your friends remember?

When they dig up your bones, as is the custom here,

will they cast them aside?

I would have tossed them into the sea,

let your spirit waft on the waves,

drift across the Atlantic to the shores of South
America, your home.


They buried you in a pauper's grave.

But you were a man rich in spirit,

a painter, a poet, a philosopher,

a wealthy man, buried in a pauper's grave.

## Small Stones:

*Small stones are everywhere. All you have to do is pause, become quiet, open your senses and allow them to appear. The final line takes you out of the mood you set in the first few lines. Here are some wrote while in Greece. 2015.*

**Athens:** *The heat is oppressive so I walk in the shadow. The pavements are like Vulcan's forge. In the trees, little birds sing.*

*Canaries trill on balconies. Through a window I hear children's voices singing a nursery song; motorcycles zoom by on the road. I wait patiently in the shade for the #25 trolley.*

**To Andrea:** *Below the high flank of the acropolis, beside the marble wall of the theatre's parados, I sit in the cool shelter of a pine tree. Here, where dramas were performed in Dionysos theatre, I meditate and wonder why, in the prime of her life, a friend should be so tragically taken.*

**The Lyceum:** *I walk through the shady gardens, past the palace there the Greek king once lived. Round a corner, and there it is – the grassy turf bared revealing walls and pathways; Aristotle's Lyceum. The palaestra where philosophers strolled imparting their knowledge; the gymnasium where young men,*

45.

*their bodies oiled and glistening, exercised in the sun. On the corner, a convoy of armed police lounge around their armoured vans.*

*The Numismatic Museum, Schliemann's house:*
*There are coins- hordes of them, finely hammered, pure gold. I find one like my ring: a silver tetra drachma with the imagine of Alexander the Great. Outside on the street, an emaciated girl holds out a cup, begging.*

*Hatzichristou Street observation: Every night at 7 pm the dog stroll beings on Hatzichristou Street. Big dogs, little dogs, stop, sniff the trees, do their doggie things, sometimes nose each other. I remember when that side of the street was apartments where some of my friends lived. Now it's the fenced backyard of the Acropolis Museum and a favorite place for the dogs evening volta.*

*The Villa Olympia:*

*If these walls could talk,*

*what would they tell me?*

*Is the Muse here?*

*Will she speak to me too?*

*The room I stay in at Villa Olympias has been occupied by a variety of writers.*

# Impressions of the Agora

A young man

saunters slowly  in the sun

playing his harmonica

as he makes he males his way

down the Sacred Way.

Distant voices

carry from the hill side.

Above me, the Acropolis

glows in golden light,

a jeweled crown on the hill.

A penned dog barks mournfully.

Distant traffic sounds blare.

But here in the Agora it is quiet.

Bees drone and butterflies

flutter about the red hibiscus

A gentle breeze stirs the branches

of the wild pepper tree.

whispers as it passes through the leaves.

Brown pods scuttle softly  to the ground


The dulcet sound of singing

carries across the empty Agora .

I am overwhelmed with sadness

Tomorrow I must leave Greece

and I wonder if I will ever return.


*Written under the wild pepper tree. Athens, October 23, 1979.*

# Songs of the Sea

# The Greek Islands: Time Suspended

I love dusty country places

where cockerels herald

the rosy dawn.

I wake to hear

the donkeys mournful brays

I love the quiet bays

where sun-dappled water

hisses and sprays

on pebbled beaches

and gulls hover, suspended

over emerald surf.


Like them

I am suspended in time

dawn, noon and evening

are serene, endless

days of golden sun

wind sighing through pines.

ring-doves cooing in eucalyptus trees.


I watch

Clouds drift silently

as passing ships

Distant islands float,

phantoms in the violet mist.

Days pass slowly, slowly.

No beginning. No end.

Time is suspended.


*Written while living in Greece in the 1980s.*

## Beach Sounds

 It takes a while, after the staccato beat of the city,

Relax into the lull of the ocean,

The shush of the waves washes away

The blare and cacophony of traffic,

The wind ruffles the beach umbrellas

The incoming surf hisses.

In no time, the hum of urban life is muted.


Then a sharp voice disturbs the tranquility,

Complains that her beach chair, which she paid for,

Is now occupied,

Her shrill voice like the call of a sea bird.

For that moment I am jolted out of the serenity,

But ah, good, a solution is found!

A moment's lull, quiet talk,

Then all is serene again.


I lay back again, let my mind drift,

soar like a gull across the sparkling sea,

The steady thrum of the waves

And hiss of splashing surf,

Washes away all other thoughts and sounds.


*Maragas Beach, Naxos Greece, 2015*

## Alone on the Beach

I don't mind that I am alone on the beach.

The sea whispers to me

The wind hums a soothing tune.

I don't mind that I am alone on the beach

I listen to the foreign voices nearby,

The Germans who hover together,

The young Swedish tourists who frolic happily in the surf

They may not notice me,

Either with a nod or a greeting

But the sea is always welcoming,

Speaks to me in a hushed voice, calming, soothing.

I don't mind being along on the beach.

I listen to the familiar cadence of the Greek beach guard

Who explains the island to the visitors.

He, of everyone, spoke to me.

"Have a good swim!"

I don't care if I'm alone on the beach

The sea is calling me,

Welcomes me in the embrace of her waves.


*Maragas Beach, Naxos Greece, 2015.*

# Finding the Muse on the Beach

A lovely beach walk from Maragas to Plaka

Quiet. Only the swish of the waves on the shore.

I'm waiting for the Muse to speak,

for the words to come.

How will I describe this beautiful shore, the serenity,

the solitude (even with other people around)?

There are tourists, not hordes.

Just those who enjoy the peacefulness and purity of
this island.

Out across the turquoise expanse, far off-shore,

Paros Island seems to drift, shrouded in mist.

There are not even any raucous gulls to disturb the
quietude.

Just the swish of the surf,

a soft rumble as breakers roll in

tossing foam on the shore.

Distant voices carried on the wind.

Quiet voices of passersby.

Footsteps, silent in the sand.

*Naxos, Greece 2015*

# Kamakis

A friend said she had to flee her island

Because of the *kamakis.*

No, they are not dangerous fish, or animals

but predators of a human kind.

I've had encounters myself back in the day

Then they were charming Adonises, hard to resist

She said her *kamakis* were 'perverts'.

I wonder, where they young or old?

Had they gone beyond the usual tactics –

A charming smile, a sexy come-on,

an invitation to dinner (which you often ended up
paying for?)

*Naxos, Greece 2015. Kamaki: A three-pronged
fishing spear. Naxos, Greece, 2015...*

# Seduction

*To Ariadne Sawyer*

*It's easy for me to understand*
how when Theseus brought Ariadne here

she ran off with the maenads

even though she had vowed her love

wen they had escaped Knossos

and the aftershock of the tsunami

when Santorini blew its top.


I have come here, like Ariadne,

enchanted by Dionysos.

He now in the form of the waiter

who brings me extra wine,

smiles, speaks I his low sensuous voice,

intrigues me.

60.

I never want to leave.

Like Ariadne, I want to flee into the hills,

leave the 'real' world,

find my own haven here

on this island of the gods, this beautiful place,

Naxos, island of my dreams.

*Naxos Greece 2015.*

## Precious Moments on the Beach

*Dedicated to the memory of little Alan Kurdi , who died on the beach at Lesbos, 2015.*

On the beach at Naxos,

It isn't just the mothers who care for their children.

Fathers tenderly cradle babies

And rock them gently as they pace the shore.

One holds his tiny daughter tight,

A mother takes her toddler's hand on their morning stroll.

Here on Naxos

Sun-browned, naked nymphs frolic at the waters edge

Children everywhere, romp in the summer sun.

Happy families together on the beach.

On another island

A child's limp body is lifted from the sand,

The shoreline strewn with abandoned life-jackets,
back-packs and debris

A father grieves for his drowned family,

A mother screams in terror.


These parents care for their children too,

Have risked their lives to escape to a 'safe' place,

Leaving the horrors of war behind


To crowd onto over-loaded rubber rafts

For a sea journey to safety.

How many of them have drowned on the voyage?

How many have lost their children

Those children they wanted to bring to a safe shore

To enjoy a future in a place where there was no war?


On Lesbos Island,

It isn't just fish the sailors catch in their nets

Brave men dive into the sea to save those who are floundering

Village women bring warm blankets, food, offer comfort.

Strangers come from afar to embrace the rescued ones.

Yet there are those who would not welcome them.

"Go back home!" they say. Home? There is no home.

It has all been destroyed, and already too many lives lost.


I sit on Naxos' shore,

Watch the happy parents stroll,

Hear the happy cries of children

And I think about that island, not too far from here

Where a frightened mother cradles her baby

And a father cries for a drowned son.

*Naxos, Greece 2015. Published in "Limitless," 2017 and on-line, 2020*

## Small Stones from the Seashore

*Naxos:* *A tiny lizard scurries up the wall under the magenta bougainvillea blossoms. The aqua swimming pool dazzles in the afternoon sun. I relax on the flagstone patio, contemplating my good fortune.*

*At Agia Ana, Naxos Greece 2015: Palms stretch out feathery fronds to embrace the wind. This oasis, the sparkling blue pool, the sun bright against whitewashed walls. The tranquility disturbed by a braying donkey and the hum of passing traffic.*

*Poseidon's horses prance on the sea, their white manes streaming over the wine-dark depths. The ship rolls and heaves. A distant island stretches out, barren and brown. White houses cluster up the hillside like pebbles strewn on the earth. The ferry ploughs ahead, rolls, shifts. I feel the coolness of sea spray on my face, blown by the wind.*

# The Colors of Zakynthos

The beach at Langana is a palette of colors.

The Ionian Sea is turquoise,

the ecru-colored beach strewn with speckled stones
and opalescent shells.

White limestone crags rise along the shore

with foliage of varied hues: pine and drab olive.

The sun is molten gold, the curtain of sky powder
blue.

The Greeks are tanned brown and flash ivory smiles.

The Brits are white, their flesh colored with black
tattoos.

The Eastern Europeans are burned red, their
children pink.


We board the glass-bottomed boat and cruise off-
shore.

Small silver fish dart among ribbons of amber seaweed.

*Caretta-caretta* turtles, green and brown,

surface out of the sea foam, lift their scaly heads, smiling.

"Sixty years old!" says the captain. "That other one's a hundred!"

The boat enters a sea cave.

The water sparkles like the multi-colored prisms of a jewel.

A girl snorkels in the crystal clear depths.

Other swimmers leap from sailboats,

frolic like dolphins in the foam-white surf.

I think of pirates who once hid in those in-dark caverns.

On Turtle Beach, where the caretta-caretta lay their eggs,

the heat scorches my feet and freckles my skin.

Signs warn "Protect area. Keep off!"

The turtles' eggs are safe from predators here

and the burning sun that cracks them open.

I roam the wave-kissed shore, pick up pearly shells,

taste salt on the cool breeze,

breathe the sweet fragrance of plants and trees,

absorb the colors of the earth, sea and sky

that paint the day, leaving a vivid image in my memory.


*Langana, Zakynthos Greece, July 2013.*

## Beach Stone, Zakynthos

Little sparrows hop around the tables and shrill in the trees. Voices surround me: Russian, Serbian, Italian, English. The beach is empty; the turquoise pool lies still. I contemplate another sunny morning on Zakynthos.

# Fair Kalliste

*"Kalliste" is the ancient name for Thira or Santorini, an island in Greece destroyed by an enormous volcanic eruption in 1400 BC and reputed by some to be the fabled Atlantis.*

The dusty olive groves

and vineyards ripe with plump red grapes

were silent, saying nothing of what was to come.

Where children played on stony beaches

below the pillared houses of the town

the turquoise sea, sun-dappled,

tossed waves upon the rocky shore.

Hephaestos' forge glowed red that day

and sent a plume of black smoke skyward

with showers of ash that gleamed

like stars in the day-bright sky.

No-one knew that soon it would

Kalliste's final hour.

The time had come

for the god's voice to speak.

Oh, fair Kalliste, with your corn stalks

tossing new green tassels in the fertile fields.

where goats graze lazily along your rocky trials,

an  young men climb the sun-drenched hillside

to watch the sunset.

Why must the gods speak out so angrily to you?

Why must they take t his paradise

and turn it back to dust?

The dying sun is bright as fire.

The sea takes its reflection

and turns to blood.

Women rock babies and hum their lullabies.

The cuckoos are not singing.

The birds have flown;

they are the first to knowledge that this will be
Kallistes' end.

Even the wind holds its breath.

Kalliste, sleep.

You will not waken in the morn.

No rosy dawn will brighten your fair hills.

The darkening sky foretells the tragic tale.

Soon black clouds will shower you

with tears of burning ash

and bury you from royal citadel

to humble cottage.

You'll lie in dust and earth

'til centuries have passed.


The earth shook

as if to tear you from its bosom.

Hephaestos' forge spewed red-hot lava

and thunderous boulders rained on you.

When 'twas done,

where city stood

and flowering fields, green groves

and ripening vines

a ragged cliff was all remained.

The sea devoured you, Kalliste.

Your cities are buried in ash.

And on the ocean's floor

lie all your treasures

lost to men forever.

New we who seek

can only wonder

why gods destroy the beauty they've created

and why men's dreams are turned to dust.

*Santorini, Greece, 1984.*

# Dora's Sunset

*In memory of my friend, Dora Preston*

The night I learned you had left us,

I walked the seaside promenade

by Poros' harbor

and paused, remembering you.

The sunset had turned the sea

into a pool of crimson

And against the blazing sky

a four-masted sailing ship

lay at anchor


I remember you, the free spirit,

You who wore purple

and buttercup yellow.

You danced in floral frocks,

amused us with funny stories

about an old lady named Clover.

I still hear your sweet voice,

singing, laughing.

I search that crimson sunset sky,

say prayers, remember you.


The next day, on Kanali beach,

I wade into the water.

A gull soars overhead,

a small white bird circles

as though it is watching me.

Is it your spirit

soaring over the blue Aegean sea?

My tears mix with the sea salt.

I hear the gentle trill of your voice,

telling me not to cry.

How could it be that you are gone,

taken from us too soon?

*Dora, you will always be remembered. Poros, Greece, June 2011.*

# Who Was That Woman Crying in the Other Room?

As the ferry pulls into Angistri's harbor

I stand on the deck, survey the familiar stretch of sandy beach.

Tranquil waves lap on the shore.

The sun is a brilliant glove over the Aegean.

My eyes are fixed on the beach-side hotel

where we had once spent happy weekends

and I wonder,

Who was that woman crying in the other room?

I remember that weekend on Angistri long ago.

You invited me to come to the isalnd...reluctantly, I thought.

but I joined you there.

Beautiful Angistri, where we so often spent weekends,

made love, walked the shaded paths along the sea.

And I still wonder...

Who was that woman crying in the other room?

I remember that weekend on Angistri

when you greeted me I had felt an iciness,

as if winter storm clouds enshrouded you

though like today, the Greek sun shone,

 bright as Agamenon's golden mask

and the lapis-colored sea sparkled with white-crested waves.

You brooded, secretive and cold.

Why had you locked your heart?

There had been no quarrel between us.

At night you turned away from me,

shunned my caresses, ignored my questions.

Who was that woman crying in the other room?

I heard he sob, "Please, don't let me go!"

You offered no explanation, no regrets

and sent me back to the city alone

without knowing, still wondering.

Now, as I stand on the ferry' deck

those memories flood back,

open the wounds in my heart.

And I still wonder:

Who was that woman crying in the other room?


*Written at the harbor of Angistri, Greece, June 2011.*

# Ballads of the Road

# Delphi's Magic

*To Kos*

I remember how you stole

pomegranates from a tree

and put them on the stone ledge

with the grapes,

sweet grapes from Delphi's vines.


We stumbled down

Parnassus' rocky slope

clambered over

shrubs and granite

to find a place to sleep

beneath the stars

 and laid among the holly oaks.

Silver lights winked

from the edge of the distant sea.

We would not know til morning

That we had made our bed

On the chasm's edge.

In night's chill

we warmed each other

The full moon shone on us

We watched meteors

shower golden trails


We felt the presence of the gods

understood the mystery

that brings men to this

Sacred shrine.

I keep these memories

forever in my heart

And every trip I make

I remember you

And the full moon

And how we were enchanted

By Delphi's magic.


*Delphi ,Greece, 1982. Published in Royal City
anthology, 2013.*

# Sanctuary

In Dion's sacred grove

in Isis Tyche's sanctuary

under the shadow

of holy Olympus,

yellow irises

tall as swords

stand in the reeds

by a silent pool.


A shepherd boy comes

whistling to his flock,

touches my arm,

says :"I'll show you how to cross the stream.

Stay away from the dogs, though.

They'll bit you here and here ."

His nimble hands

brush my breasts and backside.

Impertinent young Pan!

Thought he'd trick me.

But I know those country rogues.

I've walked this way before.


*At the Dion Archaeological site, Greece.  2005.*

# This Melancholy Road

Cruisin' along the highway.

The afternoon sun

burns away the mistakes

that clings in wisps

over empty green fields.


Rollin' along the winding road

past nameless little towns

(Where are the people?)

this sad gypsy girl

heard the bouzouki music

and dreams of gay taverna nights.

Of friends laughing and dancing,

of laurel and pomegranate trees

and crooked little streets,

marble paving stones

worn smooth by many feet of time.

Bumpin' along the melancholy road

by the granite cliffs

and autumn-bar tees

this sad gypsy girl wonders:

"Where is my home?"


*On leaving Greece, 1979.*

# The Road to Lamia

*(Macedonia, Farewell)*

The road to Lamia follows the sea,

A long stretch of narrow beach,

Water varies in color in the shallows,

turquoise, aqua, deep cerulean blue.

White caps stirred by the wind

Poseidon's prancing horses.

On the beach, fishermen

haul in nets full of fish,

shepherds tend their lazy flocks by the shore.

Sad old women dressed in black

stand by the roadside shrines

with icons, candles and incense.

Shaggy goats munch grass

under live trees, gnarled and ancient,

At Katerina, new snow on the mountains.

The late afternoon sun

shines on clouds of polished silver.

The trees are touched with rosy colors of autumn.

Craggy mountains all around.

A castle high on a hill, remnant of Crusader days.

The dying sun reflects gold

In the darkening sky.

Mist clings in the valleys.

Macedonia, goodbye.

*Greece, Oct. 1979.*

## Ode to Greek Grandmothers *(Yiayas)*

There's nothing like the Greek *yiayias.*

They hurry onto the bus, voices pitched high

off to do the day's shopping.

Most these days are stylishly dressed,

hair neatly coiffed,

wearing neatly pressed slacks

and colorful blouses.

They carry purses and two grocery carts.


In the village *yiayias* still wear the traditional
black of mourning.

They hover on porches like crows, wary of
everything.

No need for media news.

They know it all – the gossip, who's new in town,

93.

how to make the best moussaka,

where to find the greenest patches of *horta.*


They are wise, know all the village lore, collect herbs,

serve you hot *raki* and cloves for your cold.

When they spit *"Pta! Pta!"* as you pass

it's meant to ward off bad spirits.

*Yiayias* are strong, self-reliant,

even in the toughest times.


*Athens, 2017.*

# The Road to Krystos

*My friend Anne wrote this poem after a visit to my village, Lala, in the late '90s. Anne has since passed away, so I am including this in her memory, along with my poem about the village.*

Near the old Venetian bridge

On our way to Karystos

We meet a shepherd coming down for lunch

To Eresmia's tavern in the village of Lala

There she'll serve him bread, cheese, soup

And cups of thick black coffee

Afterwards he'll linger, smoking

*Kalimera*, he says

And we answer

Smiling at the way he stares at us

In our Nikes and backpacks

Foreign women on his island


Scents of basil and wild dill float

Down the mountain

And we walk past grove where oranges and lemons

Hang heavy on branches

Here's a shrine beside the road

Inside are offerings in the glassed-in case

Two cans of coke, a handful of coins

And a half bottle of red wine


There a tethered goat near a gnarled olive tree baas

Brazen he is, watching us

A car passes, its dust covering the road

He's coming from the castle, she says, pointing up

It's there, a mile or two past Lala, above the church

Sheep bells tinkle from an alpine meadow

And iridescent scarabs lift and fall into the grass

While poppies sing in red clusters

All around us


The suddenly there is a fragrance of sea salt

And a breath of wind stirs my hair

Cooling the sweat that runs in rivulets down my back


And finally—we are in Karystos

Sipping ouzo and dreaming

While we wait for the Athens ferry

To take us from this ancient place

This island called Evvia

Of which it is written

In the *Iliad*

That "men with tied back hair"

Sailed from here

To soldier in the Trojan wars.

## Lala: Return to Eden

I trudge up the familiar road  to the little mountain
village

Lala, my Garden of Eden.

A cluster of stone houses, 100 people,  and 1000
sheep.

I used to say it wasn't really a 'hamlet', just an 'omelet'.

Past the lone church, up the incline, once just a goat's
path.

I see desolate houses, shutters closed, doors boarded
up.

Once there were open windows,

village women stood on the balconies,

**waved greetings,**   *"Kali mera!* Good morning!"

Now when I call out

startled birds fly from the rooftops

Kyria Erasmia's red geraniums still bloom

in clay pots on her patio.

Where is she?

Where are all the folk


Has she gone too?

Where are all the folk

who toiled in the olive and citrus groves,

the black-clad *yiayias* with bent backs

who collected bundles of oregano

from the mountain top?

Where are the old men

who sat on verandas

sipping thick chocolate-flavored coffee?

Where are the shepherds and their shaggy flocks that

jangled up the hillsides at dawn?

I stand on the dirt road, listening.

Far away in the valley I hear a dog bark.

I listen for the cackling of hens,

a crowing rooster, the bleating of goats.

There is only silence.


Lala. The name means "chattering woman,"

The day is beautiful, bright.

Yet even the sun's golden light does not penetrate

the dismal shadow that has cast an eerie pall over the village.

There's not a living soul, not even an animal.

The iron gate concealing Antonia's courtyard is locked,

 sealing all my memories inside.

I want to go inside, walk along the familiar cobblestone path past the stone bake-oven, go up to the old wooden door,

my *spitaki*, the little house, its thick stone walls

shaded by a gnarled olive tree and grape arbor,.

I want to step onto the porch

where I slept under million of stars,

counted meteors and satellites in the night sky


That house had stood there for hundreds of years

Over the fireplace, a corner-stone is carved with a Byzantine cross. 1754.

I whitewashed  its ancient walls,

hung herbs from the rafters,

furnished it with things from Antonia's horde:

a table, two cots, a couple of chairs, an old iron bed.

Sitting on the porch in the afternoon sun

I listened to the cicadas chirring,

watch emerald green scarabs alight on the roses bushes.


Antonia said there was a ghost in the house

Her name was Evangelitsa

She died in the bed with the iron bedstead where I slept.

"She must look on you with a good eye," the village women said.

One day a cat came. I named her Miss Kitty,

To me, she was Evangelitsa's spirit.

She gave birth to a litter under the bushes in the orange grove

brought them to me, one by one,

laid them at my feet - a gift.


I want to go inside my *spitaki* once more,

visit Erasmia in her flower garden,

103.

sit with the shepherds sat under the mulberry tree,

listen to their friendly banter over glasses of *krasi*,

blush when they tease me

when I made mistakes with my elementary Greek.


I remember how I flirted secretly with Mitso while Erasmia sat knitting

pretending to be our chaperon

One night he sneaked down to visit me.

We sat on the steps giggling like teenagers.

"This is the best life," he said. "the *zoe!*"

The day I met him on the road to Karystos

he was riding his white horse,

so handsome and tanned,

That smile of his enchanted me.

"Come, marry me and live in the village," he said.

But I knew that if I did, and it failed, I'd never be able to return again.

Now they are gone, all my shepherd friends: Mitso, Themistokles, Vassilis.

I listen for their voices,

**hear only the faint, distant call of a** *kookovia*

and the mournful bray of a donkey.


I climb down the stony path to the old mill.

It is quiet and cool under the shade of the big plane trees.

The waterfall makes a soothing splash

as it tumbles from a cleft in the mountainside.

I pick a spray of myrtle,

white flowers with fuzzy stamens, dark green shiny leaves,

cross the stream on the stepping stones,

walk the dusty trail to the hillside.

A little chapel stands guard over Lala's cemetery.

Among tumbled tomb-stones and knee-high weeds,

I search for Mitso's grave,

trace my fingers over the mossy stone to find his name.

I remember then, that after five years bones are dug up,

washed in oil, placed in an ossuary

I place the myrtle wreath on the grave that now holds his sister's bones,

keep one sprig for myself.

The Greeks say if you take a sprig of myrtle home,

 it means you will return again.

There **once was so much life here,** *zoe.*

But now it seems the village has died,

and I know I can never return.

*Lala is a tiny village, 7 kms  un the mountainside
from Karystos, Euboeia (Evvia).*

*August, 2011.*

# Hymns for Gods and Heroes

The idea for *The Alexandrian Collection* was conceived in Athens when a poet friend who was critiquing my novel *The Shadow of the Lion* suggested as it is written in lyrical prose, that I should write a collection of poems based on the story.

A hymn, or *hymnos* means a form of "woven" or "spun" speech. The word "hymn". although Asiatic, derives from a Greek word for weaving, *hyphainein*. A hymn results when you intertwine speech with rhythm and song. The oldest recorded usage of the word "hymn" appears in Home's *Odyssey.* Most Homeric Hymns are composed in the hexameter. Many of them are cult-oriented.

There are sixteen hymns in the **ALEXANDRIAN COLLECTION**, and they are intended to be preformed by two voices and an accompaniment of musical instruments of that period, such as flutes, the lyra or harp and light percussion.

# Prelude

How shall I sing to you

of deities and mortals?

Shall I sing to you as a lover

or as a warrior?

How shall I sing to you

of gods and heroes?

Shall I make music

that crashes like the thunder

of Zeus' chariots

or trills as sweetly as Pan's flutes?


I will sing

of ancient shrines

with gilded temples

where mortals worship

in mysterious groves.

I will sing

of lovely Samothraki

that island sanctuary,

where cyclamen and violets

flower among the pine trees

where dancers twirl

to rhythms of drum and timbrel

and priestesses divine omens

in the ivy columned

House of the Great Gods.


First, I will sing the god's song.

# Introduction to House of the Muses

*A play in three acts, in memory of the lyric poet, Sappho.*

The story of Sappho, the lyric poet from the island of Lesbos who lived in the 5th century BC, is a classic story of betrayal and unrequited love. Sappho has been misunderstood in modern times. She was not simply a woman who wrote love poems to some of her girls. She was a widow, a mother, a woman with male lovers, and most importantly, she was a political activist and a musical super-star of her time.

This is the opening narrative from my three-act play, *House of the Muses,* the name Sappho gave for the school she ran for young girls of wealthy families. I have used some of her words and some of my own in the text and in doing so hope to make Sappho live again, exploring the challenges women have when faced with unrequited love and aging.

# House of the Muses

*(opening monologue/lyric poem)*

## Scene One

*The stage is dark. There is a faint sound of music. The lights come up slowly to reveal an idyllic tableau scene depicting Sappho's villa, the "House of the Muses". Sappho sits on the steps holding her lyre, surrounded by her girls including Atthis. The younger girls, Grynno and Timas are playing with a ball. The villa is well-kept and the scene is serene.*

*The stage lights dim and darken. The music fades. An ethereal, misty light appears over the area representing the sea and out of the mist a shimmering figure emerges. It is the Spirit of* **Sappho**, *dressed in white as a Muse, carrying her lyre. She walks slowly forward and stands in front of an altar with a statue of Aphrodite, arms raised in a supplication to the Goddess.*

### SAPPHO:

Aphrodite, weaver of wiles, Come to me here in your sacred precinct of apple trees and altars smoking with incense. I beg you, Lady, come to me now. Do not abandon me, Lady. Do not ask "What is

it this time, Sappho? Why are you calling me again?"
Do not ask "Who is wronging you now?" My heart has
been broken. Come to me, Aphrodite, release me
from my agony. When I died, I feared I would lie
forever unremembered, invisible even n the House
of Hades. Remember me. I am Sappho of Lesbos,
that island of radiant beauty, of green meadows
where horses graze, and craggy mountains fragrant
with the scent of thyme, oregano, and pine.

Plato called me the Tenth Muse. My songs and poetry
were known from this, my island, Lesbos throughout
all of the Greek world and Asia, from Egypt to the
Greek colonies in Sicily. I am Sappho, lyric poet,
singer of songs, lover, teacher, mother, and friend. I
came from a noble family. Once we owned villas,
orchards and many vineyards. When the tyrants
came to power I fought against them and they
banished me to distant Syracuse. I have been
slandered and reviled. My words torn to shreds and
buried deep in the sands of Egyptian tombs.

My rivals thought they could silence me, accused me
of forbidden love. But nothing will quench the poets
song or rob me of my words. The Muses bestowed
on me these gifts, and I have shared them with the
girls who were sent to my House of Muses: gifts of
dance, song, poetry and the art of love. But alas!
Even the Muses abandoned me. I was condemned by
my rivals, called a *corrupter of youth.* This is not the

truth. The truth is, I have loved too much...unconditionally and passionately.

*(she appeals to Aphrodite)*

Aphrodite, beautiful Lady born from the sea. I plead to you. Do not let my voice be silenced. Let the world remember me...

I am Sappho, singer of songs, lover and friend. Allow me to tell my story!

*(Sappho is again swirled in mist and retreats to the sea where she vanishes. The stage is darkened, then gradually as the lights come up.)*

*   *   *

# Biography

W. RUTH KOZAK is a published historical novel writer and travel journalist who sometimes writes poetry. Several of her poems have been published in anthologies including the most recent, "Precious Moments on the Beach" in *Limitless*, an Anthology Charity Project by McGrath House with proceeds going to refugees and immigrants. Several others have been published on-line and in anthologies. Ruth lived for several years in Greece and tries to visit nearly every year. She is currently working on a YA historical novel titled *Dragons in the Sky*, in which some of the chapters are written as Bardic verse.

## Websites

www.ruthkozak.com
www.inalexandersfootsteps.com

Manufactured by Amazon.ca
Acheson, AB

10968619R00071